Little ECO EXPERTS

Ways to Save Energy

Translated by
Diana Osorio

How to be
guardians of
the planet

PowerKiDS press

Published in 2023 by PowerKids, an Imprint of Rosen Publishing
29 East 21st Street, New York, NY 10010

Copyright © 2020 Editorial Sol90, S.L. Barcelona
All rights reserved.

No part of this book may be reproduced in any form without permission in writing from the publisher, except by a reviewer.

Cataloging-in-Publication Data
Names: Editorial Sol 90 (Firm).
Title: Ways to save energy / by the editors at Sol90.
Description: New York : Powerkids Press, 2023. | Series: Little eco experts | Includes glossary and index.
Identifiers: ISBN 9781725337169 (pbk.) | ISBN 9781725337183 (library bound) | ISBN 9781725337176 (6pack) | ISBN 9781725337190 (ebook)
Subjects: LCSH: Energy conservation--Juvenile literature.
Classification: LCC TJ163.35 W397 2023 | DDC 333.791'6--dc23

Coordination: Nuria Cicero
Editor: Alberto Hernández
Editor, Spanish: Diana Osorio
Layout: Àngels Rambla
Design Adaptation: Raúl Rodriguez, R studio T, NYC
Project Team: Vicente Ponce, Rosa Salvía, Paola Fornasaro
Scientific Advisory Services: Teresa Martínez Barchino

Imaging and infographics:
www.infographics90.com
Firms: Getty/Thinkstock, AGE Fotostock, Cordon Press/Corbis, Shutterstock.

Manufactured in the United States of America

CPSIA Compliance Information: Batch # CSPK23. For Further Information contact Rosen Publishing, New York, New York at 1-800-237-9932.

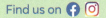

CONTENTS

What Is Energy? 4
Why We Have to Save Energy 6
The Magic of Electricity 8
What a Waste! 10
What Is Renewable Energy? 12
What Is Nonrenewable Energy? 14
What Energies Do We Consume? 16
Nuclear Energy 18
Using Waste 20
How Energy Comes Home 22
What Appliances Use the Most Energy at Home? . 24
A Matter of Watts 26
What Can You Do? 28
Good Habits to Save Energy 32
When We Are Outside 34
Capture Heat 36
Glossary 40
Index 40

WHAT IS ENERGY?

Energy is the ability to perform a job. Our bodies need energy to function and that's why we need to eat. The same is true for a light bulb, a vehicle, or a computer—they all need energy to work.

Food

All living beings get energy from the foods they eat every day. Thanks to them we can grow, think, run and more!

Fuels

Energy can be produced by burning fuels, such as wood, coal, or petroleum. The majority is obtained from nonrenewable natural resources.

Types of Energy

Driving a car, cooking food, using your tablet, turning the lights on... to do most of the activities that we perform daily, we use different types of energy.

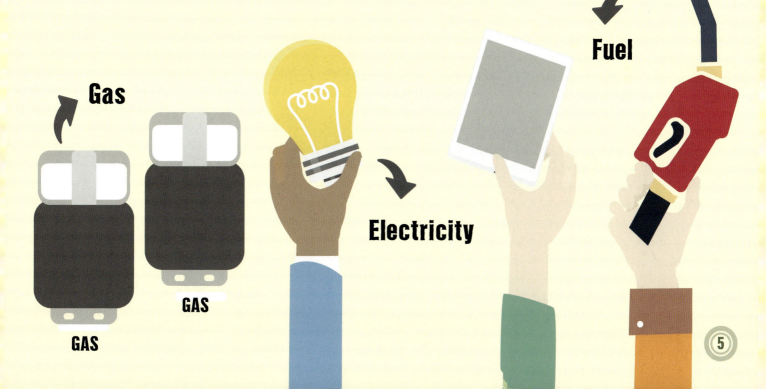

WHY WE HAVE TO SAVE ENERGY

Energy is what makes most of the things around us work: our family car, artificial lights, home appliances and so on. There are different types of energy. Find out why we shouldn't waste it.

Because It Runs Out

Energy is obtained from natural resources like petroleum, natural gas, or coal; these are nonrenewable resources. This means that if we waste this energy, we deplete the resources needed for the future.

THE GOAL

We must be efficient and look for ways to consume less energy at home.

Because It's Expensive

Energy is not free: it costs money as it is made and transported to be used in cities or in factories.

To Save the Environment

The less energy we use, the less we pollute the planet.

THE MAGIC OF ELECTRICITY

Electricity is the most used form of energy. It allows us to operate all kinds of devices, turn on lights, and so on. It is made from other types of energy—such as nuclear, solar, or hydraulic energy—which are transformed in generators.

Circuits

Electric current flows and is transformed into light, heat, force, motion, or sound. The path that this current travels in is what we call a circuit.

3 Light
This device transforms electrical energy into light and heat.

2 Conductor
Cables are made of materials that conduct electricity, such as copper.

1 Battery
It generates electricity from chemical reactions. The current flows from the positive to the negative pole.

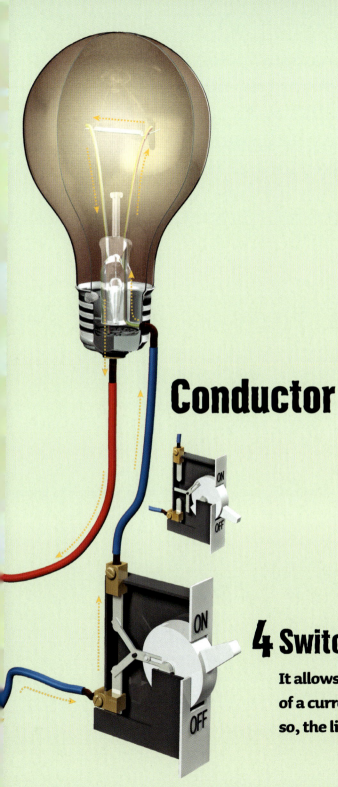

Conductor

How It Works

All circuits have an electricity generator, such as a power plant or a battery. The generator is connected to a receiving device (such as a lamp or a washing machine) by conductive wires through which the electricity flows.

4 Switch

It allows us to interrupt the flow of a current in a circuit. By doing so, the light is switched off.

WHAT A WASTE!

Today, energy consumption (by cars, lights, appliances, etc.) is so high that, in addition to polluting our planet, depletes our natural resources. Take a look at how much energy is used for different things.

At Home

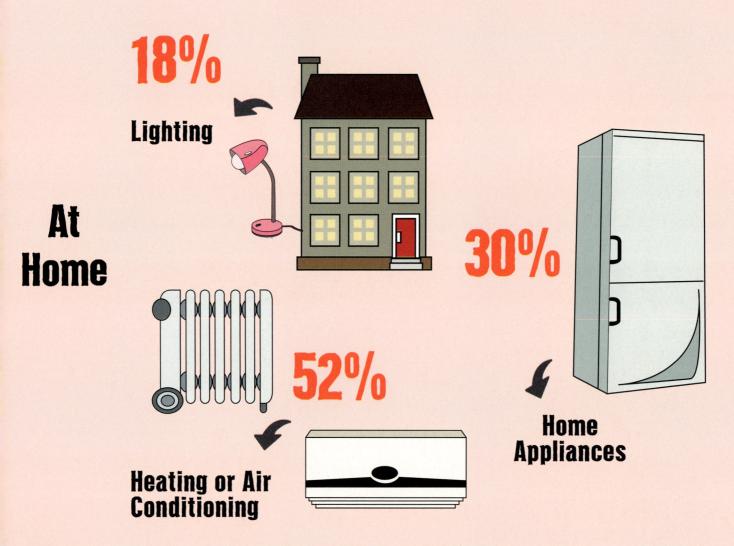

18% Lighting

30% Home Appliances

52% Heating or Air Conditioning

In the City

9%
Services for citizens

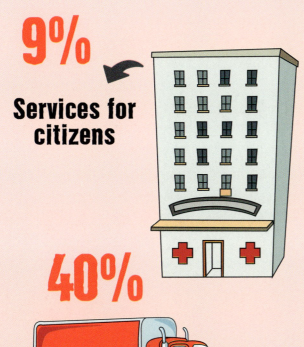

3%

Industry

40%

Transportation

4%

Farming

WHAT IS RENEWABLE ENERGY?

Hydraulic Energy

Hydroelectric power plants take advantage of the power of moving water to drive turbines that generate electricity.

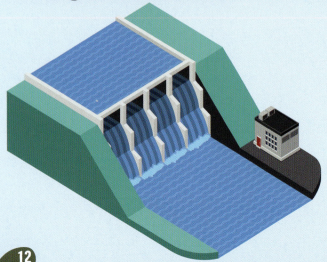

Solar Energy

The heat given off by the sun is known as solar energy. It is channeled through panels that convert heat into electrical energy.

We can distinguish between renewable and nonrenewable energy. Renewable energies are solar, hydraulic, and wind energy. They do not run out. They are also clean because they do not pollute the environment.

Wind Energy

The wind can also produce energy by moving huge windmills. These move generators that produce electricity.

Biomass

There are other types of renewable energy. For example, biomass is organic waste that is used as fuel.

WHAT IS NONRENEWABLE ENERGY?

Petroleum

It is an oily liquid extracted from underground wells. The most commonly used fuels, such as gasoline, are extracted from it.

Natural Gas

It is a mixture of hydrocarbons in a gaseous state that is extracted from underground deposits, like petroleoum, and transported in gigantic pipelines.

Nonrenewable energy comes from natural resources called fossil fuels (coal, gas, oil) that take a long time to regenerate. Another type of nonrenewable energy is nuclear energy.

Coal

It is an organic mineral that is extracted from underground mines. When burned, it generates heat energy.

Nuclear

It is obtained from the atoms of two elements, uranium and plutonium, which release great energy when they disintegrate. It is a very polluting energy.

WHAT ENERGIES DO WE CONSUME?

Petroleum is the most used fuel on the planet (32.9%). Why is that a problem? Because there are not enough reserves left and it will run out in the long term.

Coal was used to power steam engines at the beginning of the Industrial Revolution. Even today, 29.2% of the world's energy depends on it.

Although fossil fuels are nonrenewable and polluting natural resources, they are the most consumed energies in the world.

Clean renewable energies account for only 11.2% of consumption, although they are gaining ground.

Despite being the most efficient, nuclear energy only makes up 4.4% of consumption.

Natural gas is the third most used fossil fuel in terms of energy production, at 23.8%. However, few reserves remain.

NUCLEAR ENERGY

One of the most efficient methods of producing electrical energy is by taking advantage of a controlled nuclear reaction. The problem with this technology is that it creates very dangerous waste that's harmful to people and the environment.

Power Generation

In nuclear power plants, high-temperature steam is produced. This powers turbines and electric generators. A nuclear reactor produces energy, which heats the steam.

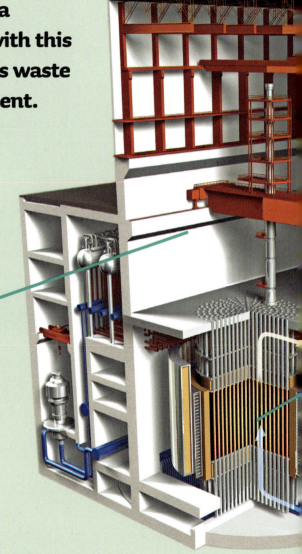

1 Mobile Crane

It moves the mechanism that refuels the nuclear fuel reactor.

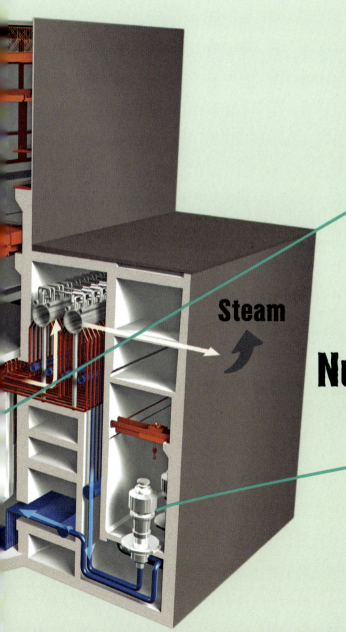

2 Reactor

It contains the radioactive fuel and is where the nuclear reaction takes place.

Nuclear Power Plant

3 Pump

It circulates fluids through the system's pipes.

USING WASTE

When bacteria break down organic material during the rotting and fermentation processes, they release biogas. This gas can be used to produce electricity and heat.

Organic Waste
This is put into a reactor and mixed with water.

Biogas
Biogas contains methane and carbon dioxide. It is used for cooking, heating homes, and producing electricity, among many other things.

Electricity

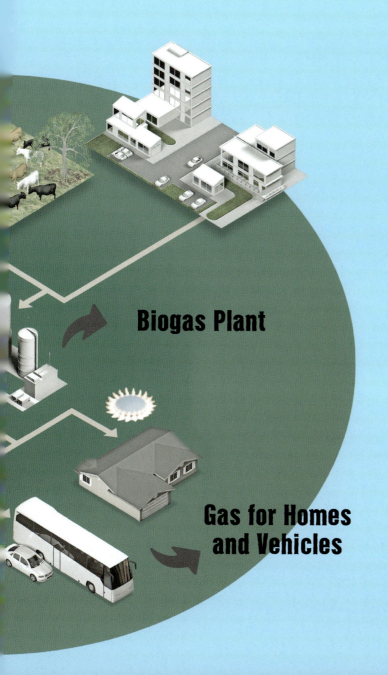

Biogas Plant

Gas for Homes and Vehicles

Reactor

It is a closed chamber like the one shown in the illustration below, where bacteria decompose organic waste.

HOW ENERGY COMES HOME

Energy is supplied to homes through different channels. If a house is not supplied with electricity, almost nothing will work.

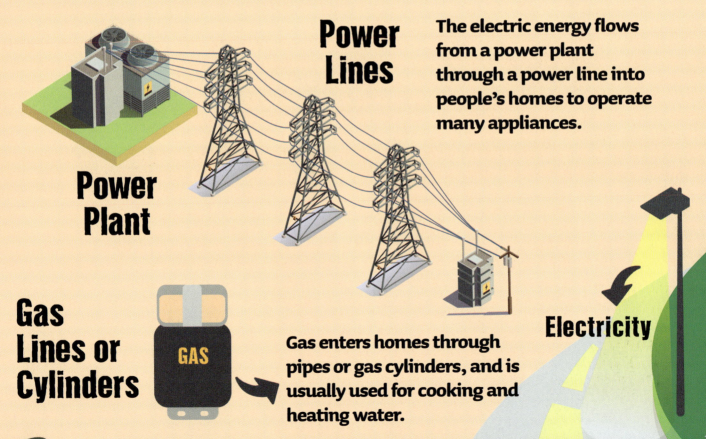

Power Lines
The electric energy flows from a power plant through a power line into people's homes to operate many appliances.

Power Plant

Gas Lines or Cylinders
Gas enters homes through pipes or gas cylinders, and is usually used for cooking and heating water.

Electricity

Solar Panels

Today, many new buildings incorporate solar panels on the roofs. The sun's energy is converted into electricity to power the building.

WHAT APPLIANCES USE THE MOST ENERGY AT HOME?

Did you know that the large and small appliances we use every day consume up to 30% of the energy that comes into a home?

Heating or Air Conditioning

50 to 70%

Appliances that generate heat or cold, such as heating and air conditioning, consume the most energy.

Dishwasher

2%

Washing Machine

8%

The lights in a house make up a large part of the energy consumed.

A MATTER OF WATTS

The energy consumed by appliances is measured in watts. That way, we can know the energy consumption of each device.

Calculate Consumption

To find out what each appliance consumes, simply multiply its power in watts by the number of hours it operates.

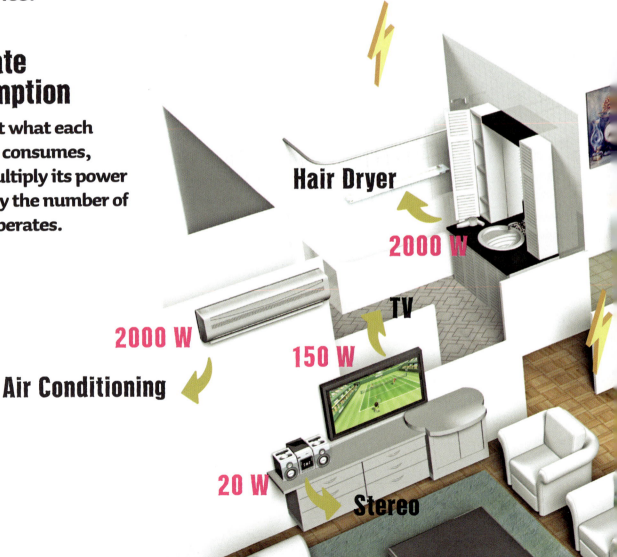

Hair Dryer — 2000 W
Air Conditioning — 2000 W
TV — 150 W
Stereo — 20 W

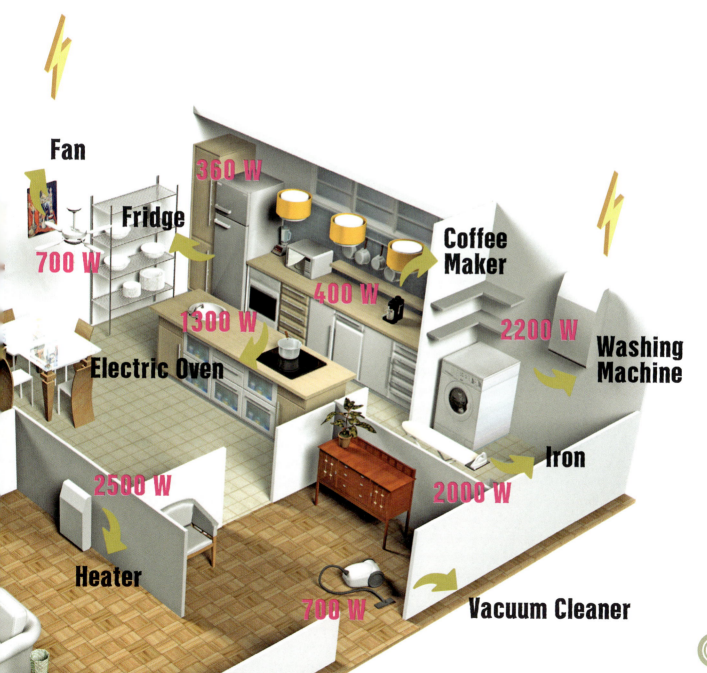

WHAT CAN YOU DO?

To keep the environment healthy and to take care of the planet, we must save energy at home. Here are 5 TRICKS to do it.

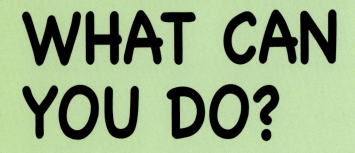

1 Always Turn Off Lights

Turn off lights when you don't need them and use energy-saving light bulbs.

2 Close the Door

Refrigerators consume a lot of electricity. Therefore, open the fridge only when you need to and try not to store hot food.

3 Fill Up the Dishwasher and Washing Machine

Always fill up these appliances. That way, both electricity and water consumption are more efficient.

4 Turn Off and Unplug the TV and Other Gadgets

Turn off the TV, computer, and gaming consoles when they are not in use. Unplug them at the wall and only plug them back in when you're ready to use them.

5 Beat the Heat

To beat the heat, keep windows and blinds closed during the day to prevent the house from heating up. If you have air conditioners or heaters, close the doors in areas of the house where these are not in use.

GOOD HABITS TO SAVE ENERGY

At Bedtime

When it's hot, use curtains or blinds to block out the sun. That way your room will be cool at night and there will be no need for a fan.

In the Shower

Turn off the water when you soap up. In addition to saving water, you save the energy that heats it up.

Throughout the day we do many things that waste energy. Take a look at these easy tricks to save energy.

In the Living Room

Disconnect the chargers of devices such as cell phones, laptops, and video consoles when the batteries are charged.

In the Kitchen

Heating up a glass of milk or food that is already cooked? Use the microwave instead of the stove. This will use less energy.

WHEN WE ARE OUTSIDE

We can contribute to energy savings and cause less pollution by following these easy tips.

Walking or Biking

If you're able to and it's not too far away, try walking or biking to school.

Walking or Biking

Not by Car

Not by Car

Cars pollute and consume gasoline. Suggest to your parents that they only use a car if all seats are occupied.

Public Transportation

Use Public Transportation

More people on public transportation means fewer people using their cars, less pollution, and more gas savings.

DID YOU KNOW?

Electric cars run on a rechargeable battery and pollute less than gasoline engines.

CAPTURE HEAT

This experiment will show you how the thermal insulation of a house works. By adjusting curtains, for example, we conserve heat in the winter and coolness in the summer.

YOU WILL NEED:
- Pencil and labels
- 4 jars
- Newspaper
- Rubber bands
- Old cotton T-shirt
- Towel
- Big box
- Thermometer

STEP BY STEP: Find the experiment steps on the next page!

STEP ONE

Wrap one of the jars with newspaper and secure it with the rubber bands.

STEP TWO

Repeat with the second jar using the T-shirt and the third jar using the towel.

STEP THREE

Label each of the jars with the letters A, B, and C.

STEP FOUR

Label one jar with the letter D and leave it inside the box. Fill in the empty spaces with paper.

STEP FIVE

Carefully fill all the jars except jar D with boiling water and close them. Leave jar D empty.

STEP SIX

After half an hour, measure the room's temperature and compare it to the temperature of each jar.

STEP SEVEN

Record how long it took for each jar to reach room temperature. Repeat the experiment using ice water. Compare the results.

Conclusion

The jar that retained the hot water the longest was the one that was best insulated. This prevents heat from escaping because a layer of air is created between the outside air and the heat inside.

Glossary

bacteria: tiny creatures that can only be seen with a microscope

biogas: a mix of the gases methane and carbon dioxide released from bacterial decomposition and used as fuel

energy: power used to do work

environment: the natural world in which plants and animals live

generator: a machine that uses moving parts to produce electrical energy

natural resources: things in nature that can be used by people

nonrenewable: not capable of being replaced

renewable: capable of being replaced

Index

electricity, 8–9, 12–13, 20, 22–23, 30

energy consumption, 10–11, 16–17, 24–25, 26–27

environment, 7, 13, 18, 28

nonrenewable energy, 4, 6, 13, 14–15, 16, 17

nuclear energy, 15, 17, 18–19

pollution, 7, 10, 13, 15, 17, 34–35

renewable energy, 12–13, 17